Contents

Acknowledgements

This book does not present a completely new concept of art and design education, but has been written to outline approaches which might be of use to teachers in the planning of their projects. It draws on a variety of reference material and I am indebted to many authors of books and papers on the teaching of historical, critical and contextual studies who have published in this country and in America. I am also extremely grateful to my colleagues in education who have discussed with me over the past few years some of the suggestions offered here.

My special thanks are due to Joe Connolly and Dr. Anthony Dyson for their advice and helpful suggestions.

Frederick Palmer
1990

Art and Design

in Context

Frederick Palmer

Longman
London and New York

Longman Group UK Limited
Longman House, Burnt Mill, Harlow,
Essex, CM20 2JE, England
and Associated Companies throughout the World.

© Frederick Palmer 1990

First published 1990
ISBN 0 582 03923 1

Set in 11/13 point Bembo (Linotron)
Produced by Longman Group (FE) Ltd
Printed in Hong Kong

British Library Cataloguing in Publication Data
Palmer, Frederick, 1936–
  Art and design in context.
  1. Graphic arts – Manuals
  I. title
  760'.028

  ISBN 0-582-03923-1

Library of Congress Cataloging in Publication Data
Palmer, Frederick
  Art and design in context / Frederick Palmer.
    p.   cm.
  Includes bibliographical references.
  ISBN 0-582-03923-1 : £9.95
  1. Art — Study and teaching.   2. Design — Study and
teaching.   I. Title.
N85.P35   1990   90-30604
707 — dc20   CIP

Cover photograph: prayer rug, India, Mughal period,
early seventeenth century. Thyssen-Bornemisza
Collection, Lugano, Switzerland.

To Eunice

Approaches to Contextual Studies

'Participation and appreciation are complementary aspects of art education: not one or the other, but both.'

The Arts in Schools – Gulbenkian Report 1982

Art and design education in schools has been centred, until fairly recently, on the practice of the subject: the acquisition of skills, the visual expression of a personal response to an idea or experience, the production of artefacts. Limited time has ensured that teacher and student concentration has been given to the requirements of a practical examination. Where the study of works of past and contemporary practitioners has occurred it has usually been under the separate title of Art History and has been considered as an academic subject, the teaching of which has been geared to an examination based on conventional notions, that is, a chronological study of period, school or movement, more often than not firmly rooted in the Western European fine art tradition. That such an approach was of interest to only a limited number of students is not surprising for it had little to do with the experience, background or interests of the majority of those attending secondary schools. There was rarely a connection between the study of art history and the practical work done in the studio, nor was there much that was of relevance to a young person living in a multicultural society such as Britain is today.

Such a limited outlook on art and design education is now less prevalent and teachers are appreciating the benefits of planning courses in which theory and practice are related. Two influences are mainly responsible for this change. These are: the Critical Studies in Art and Education Project and the General Certificate of Secondary Education. Between September 1981 and the Summer of 1984 the Critical Studies in Art and Education Project was run by Rod Taylor with the sponsorship of the School Curriculum Development Council, the Crafts Council and the Arts Council of Great Britain. That such organisations should be prepared to support a programme of research into the relationship between the practical and theoretical aspects of art and design is indicative of the importance which critical/contextual studies were assuming in the eyes of those involved in art and design education.

In his account of the CSAE Project, *Educating for Art* (Longman 1986) Rod Taylor chronicles the project's progress with descriptions of the students' reactions to the work of past artists and the relationships between contemporary art and their own endeavours. He gives evidence, often in the student's own words, of the importance of their experiences not just to their current work, but to their creative development and consequently to their lives in general. The findings documented in the book made a strong case for critical/contextual studies to be a part of every student's art and design education. The publication of the first documents related to the GCSE reinforced this notion, stressing the importance of linking theory and practice in ways which would enable students to gain an appreciation of historical, cultural, social, religious, political and economic contexts in which art and design has been and is being created and to see their own work in relation to that of others.

The requirements of the GCSE have brought to the attention of those involved in art and design education, aspects which we all know to be part of the subject, present in the work of many art departments, but not always dealt with in the most constructive way. With the national criteria and the syllabus details published by the various examination groups, good practice has been brought together, tabulated in a logical manner and presented to teachers not as a newly discovered way of working, but as a clearly defined list of objectives and working methods. These should be included in any art and design syllabus in a structured manner and should not be dealt with haphazardly.

One of the new examination's recommendations is for contextual studies to be part of every student's course. It should be an integral part of it, not a separate component, except at the mature level. Consequently, the plans for a syllabus, the aims of projects, the suggested working procedures should not be decided upon without consideration of the contextual studies element. The practical and the theoretical must now be intertwined and their relationship considered at all times from the initial stages of course planning to the final assessment and evaluation.

Any work undertaken should relate theory and practice with each helping the other, as part of a programme which is planned so that the student learns in a logical manner without unnecessary repetition. As with any course, contextual studies should take account of the student's needs, abilities and interests. What the student knows is a sound basis for extending ability and understanding.

Obviously, there is no one correct way of dealing with contextual studies. The interests and expertise of students and teachers will influence the decision about how to approach the subject, how to relate it to the practical work, how to make it an integral part of the art and design department programme, and how best to make it relevant to the student's educational experience.

For obvious reasons this book cannot provide a course of study appropriate for all students at all stages. What it aims to do is to outline some approaches to the teaching of contextual studies and suggest five project-based courses, not as exemplars to be taken and used as presented, but as illustrations of possibilities upon which teachers can build. They are starting points from which variations catering for individual requirements can be devised.

Contextual studies is not a new name for art history, that part of the art curriculum which so often dealt with fine art within the framework of such courses as; 'From Caves to Cubism', 'Pre-History to Picasso' or 'Giotto to Cézanne'; although it needs to be said that a sense of history, of events and achievements in time, is inevitable and desirable. Contextual studies is about making links across cultures as well as within our own; learning to appreciate how ideas have been developed, feelings expressed and problems solved by people in different countries and at different times. European art and design may be the core rather than a specialist area of study in isolation.

No course or project can deal with everything at once and so the approach will have to be selected according to the learning experience desired, and the area of study being undertaken. The following list gives a number of possible approaches in an attempt to simplify the problems. It is not exhaustive and may easily be extended in response to individual needs and interests. Such a list of categories does not mean that each is independent of the other. Whatever the main emphasis, there will often be other attributes contained within it, sometimes obviously, at other times extracted as the work progresses.

Possible areas of study

Listed under the following headings are indicators of possible areas of study and not detailed descriptions of the titles.

1 **Chronological** – historical survey, possibly thematic, e.g.
   - a study of the art and design of a culture;
   - country;
   - artist;
   - designer;
   - craftsperson;
   - theme;
   - medium or technique.

2 **Comparative** – different approaches, interpretations, expressions or solutions, e.g.
   - a study of the similarities and differences between the works of different cultures;
   - countries and artists;
   - interpretations of themes;
   - solutions to visual problems;
   - representations of the world and methods of visual communication.

3 **Formal** – considerations of the visual elements of art and design. In addition to the visual elements of art and design other formal aspects of the subject could be taken as project themes, e.g.
   - structure;
   - pictorial composition;
   - two and three-dimensional studies;
   - movement;
   - rhythm;
   - visual rhyme and repetition;
   - harmony and contrast.

4 **Imaginative** – symbols, inventions, fantasies, e.g.
   - representations of heaven and hell;
   - the future;
   - illustrations to fantasies, e.g. *Ramayana*, *The Thousand and One Nights*, *Sir Gawain and the Green Knight*, *Superman*, *Star Wars*, and science fiction stories.

5 Social – social, cultural, geographical, religious, political and economic issues, e.g.

- art and propaganda;
- public patronage;
- art in our community;
- art and mass entertainment;
- art and the women's suffrage movement;
- art and industry;
- art and education;
- the portrayal of women;
- the portrayal of men;
- the depiction of people from other cultures;
- freedom and oppression;
- visual cliché and stereotypes.

6 Themes and variations, e.g.

- figures in the landscape;
- movement;
- windows;
- distortion;
- reflection;
- spirals;
- or particular paintings with variations by other artists, e.g. Le dejeuner sur l'herbe, Las Meninas, Femmes d'Alger.

7 Individuals – the study of individual artists, designers, crafts-people, architects.

As well as studying the obvious examples of artists from Western European art such as Leonardo da Vinci, Cézanne and Picasso, there are also artists from other cultures to consider, e.g.

- K'un Ts'an, the seventeenth century Chinese artist;
- the seventeenth century Mughal painters, Mushfig and Abu'l hasan Nadir-el-Zaman (the wonder of the age);
- Japanese eighteenth and nineteenth century print makers such as Hiroshige, Utamaro and Hokusai;
- the twentieth century Mexican artist, Diego Rivera;
- contemporary Caribbean painters and black artists working in Britain and the USA.

In addition the numerous designers, craftspeople and architects from different ages and cultures should not be forgotten. Patrons of the arts could also be the subject of a project, e.g. the Medicis, Suleyman the Magnificent, Popes, the Doges of Venice, the Steins, Paul Getty, Douglas Cooper and contemporary patrons.

8 National Schools of Art, e.g.

- Italian;
- British;
- Dutch;
- French;
- Japanese;
- Rajasthan Kishangarth School.

9 Art movements, e.g.

- Mannerism;
- Romanticism;
- Realism;

- Impressionism;
- Cubism;
- Surrealism;
- de Stijl;
- Constructivism;
- American Expressionism.

10 Key works (in Western Art), e.g.
- Discobolus;
- The Madonna of Chancellor Rolin – van Eyck;
- Las Meninas – Velasquez;
- The Third of May – Goya;
- Olympia – Manet;
- Impression, Sunrise – Monet;
- Les Demoiselles d'Avignon – Picasso;
- Nude Descending a Staircase – Duchamp;
- Unique Forms of Continuity in Space – Boccioni;
- Campbell Soup Cans – Warhol.

11 Popular culture, e.g.
- television;
- photography;
- film;
- newspapers;
- magazines;
- comics;
- fairgrounds;
- amusement arcades;
- carnival costume;
- masks;
- puppets;
- dolls;
- models;
- souvenirs;
- ceramic figures;
- flower arrangement;
- custom cars;
- house decoration.

12 Media studies, e.g.
- advertising;
- word and image;
- graphic design;
- sound and image.

13 Visual and performing arts – relationships and contrasts, e.g.
- art and design, music, drama, dance;
- projects on specific productions;
- aspects of masque, circus, carnival, pantomime, opera, ballet, film, video;
- joint projects on such themes as Time, Space, Movement, Structure, Repetition, Pattern, Reality and Illusion.

14 Art and science, e.g.
- botanical and biological illustration;
- anatomical and medical illustration;

- drawing systems;
- charts and diagrams;
- cartography;
- natural and man-made structures;
- photography;
- computer imagery.

15 Monocultural studies, e.g.
- Europe;
- Africa;
- India.

16 Multi-cultural – different interpretations of a theme, e.g.
- the portrayal of women in Japanese and French nineteenth century print-making;
- flowers in English embroidery and Indonesian batik;
- animals in European heraldry and Indian miniature painting;
- non-figurative imagery in Christian, Jewish and Islamic art.

17 Male and female artists, e.g.
- Rosa Bonheur and Meissonier;
- Cassatt and Degas;
- Lee Miller and Max Ernst;
- Morisot and Manet;
- arts and crafts movement;
- designers and craftspeople.

18 Private and public art and design, e.g.
- murals;
- roadsigns;
- graffiti;
- equestrian statues;
- neon signs;
- posters.

19 Art, craft, design and technology, e.g.
- graphic and industrial design;
- links with technology;
- computer graphics;
- furniture;
- textiles;
- architecture.

20 Two and three-dimensional studies, e.g.
- drawing;
- engraving;
- painting;
- printed textiles;
- embroidery;
- film, video, photography;
- sculpture;
- architecture;
- ceramics;
- woven textiles;
- construction;
- performance arts.

Five Project-based Courses

In some respects the first five headings on the list on pages 7–8 could be taken as the main approaches under which all the other suggestions might be placed. Perhaps too, other approaches not listed could also be allocated places under these main headings for they do, to a large extent, cover the broad areas within which contextual studies might be placed. It is for this reason that I have taken them as the basis for the five courses outlined here. Whilst elements of the remaining approaches given in the list will be seen to appear from time to time, no attempt has been made to introduce them all. Their inclusion is simply evidence of further possibilities. The five project-based courses are:

Chronological – The Family
Comparative – Space
Formal – Pattern
Imaginative – Dreams
Social – Parades

Where possible it will be advantageous to study real paintings, sculptures, architecture and artefacts and so visits to museums, galleries, churches, libraries and other locations will be an important part of the student's research programme. However, secondary source material in the form of books, reproductions, postcards, slides, photographs, film and video recordings will be essential.

Many of the areas of study listed under one theme are transferable to one or more of the others, but, for obvious reasons, have not been repeated. They should be considered as suggestions for exploration or trigger mechanisms for other ideas rather than prescriptive topics or definitive coverage of the theme.

Each of the five themes in the book could be studied in a number of ways common to all. For example, emphasis could be placed on the following:

- Eurocentric interpretations;
- cross-cultural interpretations and links;
- mass media presentation;
- social and religious contexts;
- relationships between fine art and popular art;
- relationships between communication and decoration;
- relationships between commerce and propaganda;
- two-dimensional and three-dimensional interpretations.

11

Chronological

The Family

Aim

To produce a two-dimensional picture, for example, by creating a painting or a photographic montage using the student's own images of people and objects which interpret the theme in a personal way. This may mean concentrating upon a contemporary family, making a chronological study of one specific family or inventing a family which spans history.

Objectives

1 To make analytical drawings and, if desired, to compose, light and create photographs of people and locations for a personal interpretation of the theme.
2 To compose a two-dimensional image with an emphasis on the use of shape, e.g. positive, negative, counterchange and overlap.
3 To learn about pictorial composition from the work of other artists and to apply that knowledge to the practical work.
4 To research the theme chronologically and consider how the grouping, costume and pictorial composition communicate ideas of culture, age, gender and social position.
5 To understand something of the contexts in which works on the theme were created; by whom, for whom and why.

Primary source material

The nature of this theme will probably mean that homework will play a key role at the start of the project. Students could be asked to draw members of their family, to take colour notes and photographs and to make decisions about the costumes worn and the locations in which the figures are to be placed. If possible, video recordings could be made of aspects of family life e.g. the making of a meal, the eating of a meal with the transformation of the table, the clearing up afterwards, an evening at home, Sunday morning, etc.

Given the difficulties of homework, it will be sensible also to re-source the project in the school art room. Costumes could be hired from outside agencies or borrowed, along with a selection of props, from the drama department. Some might be brought in by colleagues as well as by the students themselves. Settings, both interior and exterior, could be created with students (singly or in pairs) posing for short periods. In this way students could make drawings and take colour notes for their figure compositions, selecting different view-points and sections of the collected material to make their personal interpretation.

Discussion

Why has the theme been selected?

1 Family grouping is almost a universal characteristic of animals and human beings. Why might this be so?
2 Most people belong to some sort of family grouping and therefore first-hand research is available.
3 Family is a word which need not always refer to a nuclear family, but may indicate different groups of people. Even those not currently in a conventional family unit will probably have a group and/or a history to which they can refer.
4 The theme has been interpreted in numerous ways in many cultures and countries throughout history. Therefore, a chronological study is possible.

The aim and objectives of the project should be explained and discussed.

1 How might we describe the theme, its meanings and its possible interpretations?
2 What images does the theme evoke in our minds?
3 What are our experiences of the theme: a) personal, and b) through other people's representation in paintings, sculpture, film, television, advertising, magazines and comics?
4 What conventional portrayals of the theme do we know?
5 Do we know any different ones? If so, when and where did they or do they occur? Why are they unconventional?
6 Why might the nuclear family be such a commonly occurring form of grouping?
7 What stereotyped presentation of the theme do we know? Why might these be so produced?

Contextual Studies

A broad chronological survey of the theme in the history of art is not being proposed. What is suggested is that a period of time or an aspect of the subject is selected in relation to the student's interests and approach to the practical work, that a chronological study is undertaken so that changes may be appreciated and placed in an historical, cultural, social, religious, political and economic context. In other words, the works studied will not be seen as art objects in isolation, but in relation to people.

Areas of Study

Areas of study could include investigations of the portrayal of the family in:

- one country, e.g. Britain, Holland, India, Italy;
- one historical period, e.g. the Romanesque;
- one medium or process, e.g. drawing;

- one school of painting or sculpture, e.g. French (Chardin to Impressionism?);
- one religion, e.g. Christianity;
- different religions, e.g. Christianity, Hinduism, Islam;
- the Holy Family theme, e.g. Nativity, Flight to Egypt, Childhood of Christ;
- popular art, e.g. prints, postcards, china figurines, magazine illustrations, dolls, toys, pub signs, Victorian engravings;
- the mass media, e.g. advertising, television, film, newspapers, magazines, comics;
- propaganda, e.g. Russian, Chinese, Mexican social realism;
- photography, e.g. an historical survey: Victorian photography to the present day;
- visual narratives, e.g. Assyrian reliefs, Egyptian murals, William Hogarth, magazine photo-stories, television soap-operas, film, theatre, comic strips.

Other approaches might include consideration of:

- the role of women in the family;
- royal families;
- merchant families;
- poverty and the family;
- stages and ages, e.g. birth, childhood, schooldays, adolescence, marriage, middle age, old age, death;
- family signs and symbols, e.g. heraldry, crests, flags, shields, badges;
- tomb sculpture and brass memorial plaques;
- personal choice, i.e. a selection made from what is liked and what is available from firsthand experience.

In addition to the aims, objectives, primary source material, proposed discussion points and the suggestions for contextual studies which are given with each project, there are three other essential aspects of any course of work. These are: synthesis, development and evaluation. The general comments which follow under these headings are relevant to the five projects in the book, but are not reprinted in each section.

Synthesis

This is the stage following the initial discussions, the analytical work from primary source material and the related research in contextual studies when the student brings together the various experiences and studies to create an individual interpretation.

The production of the final piece or pieces of work should be the result of a learning process, not a 'one-off' statement. The student may have studied one aspect of the project theme in depth or dealt with material from disparate sources. But whichever approach, what should be apparent is a progression of ideas showing evidence of analysis and investigation, a willingness to extend original conceptions and an ability to bring together into a personal statement the results of research and invention. Visual and verbal evidence of related contextual studies should be a part of the student's final statement and be considered an integral part of the evaluation and assessment.

Development

For some students a development into other media might be desirable. For example, an extension from a drawing or painting into three-dimensional construction, textiles, graphics, print, photography or video with a related programme of contextual studies running alongside.

Consideration could also be given to the advantages of cross curricular links which would allow the student to develop a more fully realised programme of work than is usually possible. An element of self-directed study will probably be present in such instances with students helping to plan their own projects and seeking advice for their research from different subject teachers in the school. The themes presented here will allow for links to be made with a number of subjects, e.g. mathematics, English, history, geography, social studies, religious education and drama.

Evaluation

General discussion concerning to what degree the aims and objectives of the project have been achieved could be undertaken in conjunction with the individual's self-assessment. Issues to be considered for evaluation and self-assessment would include comment on the following:

1 Motivation. The understanding of, and reponse to, the project requirements, aims and objectives.
2 Use of resources.
3 Response to primary sources. Observation and visual analysis.
4 Response to secondary sources. Research and use of reference materials.
5 Use and understanding of formal elements.
6 Use and understanding of materials.
7 Selection of appropriate working procedures, media and techniques.
8 Extension of ideas through considered working processes into a final statement.
9 Personal interpretation (including technical skills).
10 Critical analysis and contextual appreciation.
11 Organisation.
12 Confidence.

Aspects of the theme

Family snapshot.

Marriage

Wedding photograph. c.1930.

The Wedding of Lord Murgan. Ceiling painting. Sri Mariamman Temple, Singapore.

Marriage a la Mode II (shortly after the Marriage). William Hogarth. c. 1743. Oil on canvas. 69.9 × 90.8 cm. National Gallery.

Infancy

The Nativity. Late twelfth century. Cotton manuscript. French or Flemish. British Library.

The Cradle. Berthe Morisot. 1872.
Oil on canvas. 54 × 46 cm.
Louvre, Paris.

The Flight to Egypt. Twelfth century.
Gislebertus. Stone carving. Autun
Cathedral, France.

Parents and children

A Family Group. Attributed to Michiel Nouts. c.1656. Oil on canvas. 178 × 235 cm. National Gallery.

Daddy, what did you do in the Great War? First World War poster. Imperial War Museum.

Public families

The Royal Family at Balmoral.
1972. Photograph by Patrick
Lichfield (Camera Press).

Billy Connolly and Pamela
Stephenson with baby Amy.
1986. Photograph by Richard
Slade (Camera Press).

The Family of Darius before Alexander. Paolo Veronese (1528–1588). Oil on canvas. 236.2 × 474.9 cm. National Gallery (E.T. Archive).

Family at work

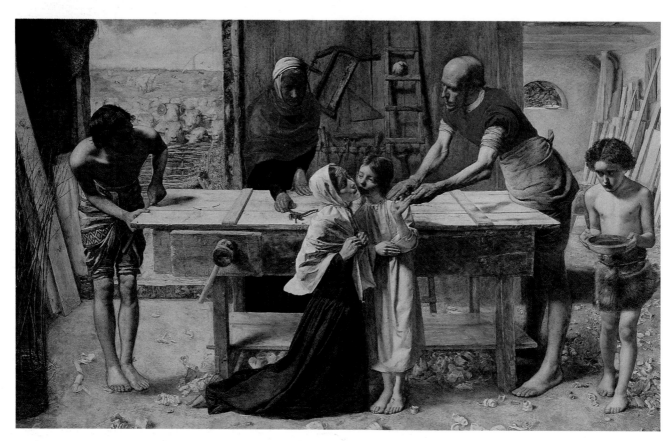

Christ in the House of His Parents. John Everett Millais. 1850. Oil on canvas. 86.4 × 139.7 cm. Tate Gallery, London (E.T. Archive).

Family at play

Mother and Children.

Wealth and the family

A Lady and Gentleman Taking Coffee with Children in a Garden. Nicholas Lancret (1690–1743). Oil on canvas. 88.9 × 97.8 cm. National Gallery (E.T. Archive).

The Murphy Family. Dorothy Russell. 1985. Oil on canvas. 91.5 × 122 cm. Collection of the Murphy Family.

and Sunset. Photograph by Henry Peach Robinson. 1885. Composite photograph from three
ves. Royal Photographic Society (The Barbican Art Gallery).

Death

Monument to Bridget Paston (died 1598) with eight of her ten children. Sixteenth century alabaster. Tittleshall Church, Norfolk.

The Resurrection-Reunion of Familes. Stanley Spencer. 1945. Oil on canvas. 76.2 × 101.6 cm. Dundee Art Galleries and Museums.

Comparative

Space

Aim

To produce a drawing in a chosen medium, or mixture of media, which communicates the three-dimensional form of an arranged still-life group.

Objectives

1 To solve the problem of how to represent space by using more than one known convention.
2 To study ways in which different cultures at different times have represented space on a two-dimensional surface.
3 To research into how different disciplines represent space, e.g. architecture, graphic design, industrial design, engineering, cartography, urban planning; and to apply this, if considered appropriate, to the practical work.
4 To gain some understanding about why different methods are used for different purposes and are, or have been employed, in other cultures and countries as well as our own.
5 To appreciate that Western European perspective is only one of many ways in which spatial elements may be presented on a flat surface.

Most of the students will have produced work in which more than one convention has been used. At its simplest, this project will allow for an appreciation of these conventions and for development whilst other students will explore unfamiliar ways of representing space, and after experimenting, decide which combinations they think appropriate solutions to the problem.

Primary source material

Some students will have sufficient difficulty deciding how to communicate the three-dimensional character of a given still-life group without the problem being magnified by the assembling of complex or intricate objects. A simple grouping of, in the main, geometrical forms might be advisable. This does not mean that a boring collection of cylinders, spheres, and cones and cubes should be presented, but that objects of simple form which will nonetheless arouse interest should be gathered together, perhaps with the students' participation.

In addition to the familiar objects to be found in the studio, items similar to those which appear in so many Cubist still life paintings and collages could be collected, e.g. a compotier of fruit, an old soda syphon, newspapers, a guitar, flute or recorder, sheet music, a checked or tasselled tablecloth. These could be updated for added interest with unusual fruit and vegetables from the Caribbean and the Orient, *Soda Stream* equipment, cassette players, sound and video tapes, records and patterned plastic cloths and formica. Alternatively, for some students a more complex group could be assembled (perhaps thematically) which would reflect particular interests, e.g. cosmetics, shoes, handbags, food, computer hardware, parts of motorbikes or cars, and sports equipment and other articles reflecting student hobbies.

In order to reduce the difficulties, the still-life group could be in shades of one colour or a selected range of colour so that not only would the spatial problems be the real focus of attention (in a manner similar to how the Cubists limited their colour range during their analytical phase), but also to allow for additional points about colour, harmony, hue and key to be taken up at an appropriate time.

Discussion

Why has the theme been selected?

1 How to represent space on a two-dimensional plane has been one of the main concerns of artists over the centuries.
2 Different countries and cultures have devised a number of conventions for communicating ideas about space and so a comparative study can be made.
3 Space can be communicated by means other than optical illusion and these methods are as valuable a part of art and design education as traditional notions of linear and aerial perspective.
4 The theme allows for experiment and a personal choice in selecting what means to use in order to solve the problem of space representation.

The aim and objectives of the project should be explained and discussed.

1 Why might we wish to represent space in a picture?
2 What ways do we know of representing space?
3 What methods are used to represent space in art and design, in geography, mathematics, history, science, design technology?
4 What are the similarities and differences?
5 Do we know of other examples from different times and countries?
6 What are the attributes and deficiencies of the different methods?
7 What methods can be used to represent the solidity of three-dimensional forms in space, e.g. light and shade, colour?

Contextual Studies

A comparative study of the theme is proposed so that students may make decisions about which conventions for the representation of space to use in solving the set problem. In addition, a consideration of various methods of space representation will involve the art of other cultures and times as well as some of the relationships between drawing, painting and the visual methods of other disciplines. For example, how was space shown in India, Africa, China and Japan at the time when Leonardo da Vinci and Paolo Uccello were experimenting with aerial and linear perspective in Europe? How have different drawing systems influenced artists such as Juan Gris, Pablo Picasso, David Hockney and Anthony Green?

Areas of Study

A comparative study of the theme could include:

- the position of people, objects and location details on the picture-plane;
- the scale of different items on the picture-plane;
- overlapping shapes;
- colour as an indication of space;
- tone as an indication of space;
- aerial perspective;
- linear perspective;
- multiple viewpoints;
- projection systems;
- chiaroscuro.

Aspects of the theme

Position

Paddy Fields near Ubud, Bali. W. Rana. 1985. Oil on canvas. 67 × 87 cm. Private collection.

Glassmaking. Fifteenth century drawing. Bohemia. British Museum.

Tone

Le Flageolet. Gavarni.
Lithograph. 20 × 15 cm. Private
collection.

St. James's Palace. W. W. Hooper
c.1867. Photograph. Royal
Geographical Society.

Colour

Harvest, Le Pouldu. Paul Gauguin. 1890. Oil on canvas. 73 × 92 cm. Tate Gallery, London.

Drawing from a Chinese album. Kung Hsien (d.1689). University of Durham, Gulbenkian Museum of Modern Art (Bridgeman Art Library).

Scale

British Army Ceremonial.
Christopher Clark poster. 1932.
British Rail. Courtesy of the
Tindale Collection.

Overlap

*Baz Bahadur and Rupmati Riding
in a Forest.* Late eighteenth
century. Gouach. 20.9 ×
15.8 cm. Sheffield City Art
Galleries.

Linear perspective

Panoramic View of London from St. Paul's. c.1850. Steel engraving. 30 × 56 cm. Plate renovated and printed by Anthony Dyson.

Interior of a Gothic Church. Peeter Neeffs (active 1605). Oil on panel. 54.4 × 85.7 cm. By permission of the Governors of the Dulwich Picture Gallery.

False Perspective. William Hogarth. The Fotomax Index, London.

Aerial perspective

Flemish Fair. Jan Brueghel. Oil on copper. 47.6 × 68 cm. Reproduced by Gracious Permission of Her Majesty the Queen.

Multiple viewpoints

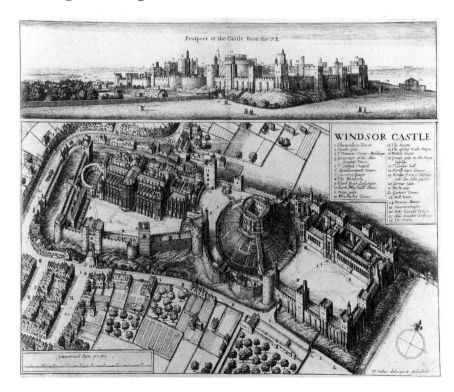

Elevation and aerial view – Windsor Castle. W. Hollar. British Museum.

The Pool in Nebamun's Garden.
1400BC. Egyptian wall painting.
Height: 64 cm. British Museum.
(Photograph: Michael Holford).

Noah's Ark. Late thirteenth
century miniature in north
French style. Hebrew Bible and
Prayer Book. British Library.

George, Blanche, Celia, Albert and Percy. Photograph by David Hockney. 1983. 120 × 190.5 cm. Photo collage © David Hockney.

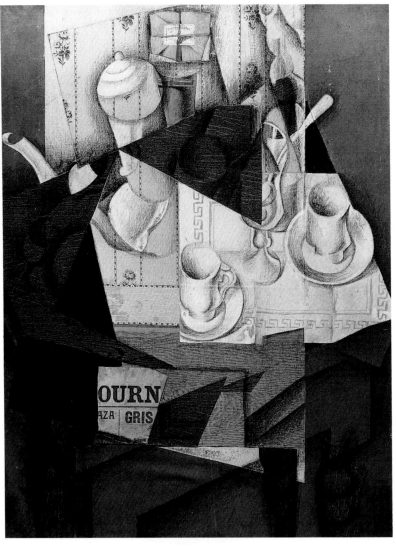

Breakfast. Juan Gris. 1914. Oil and collage on canvas. 80.9 × 59.7 cm. Museum of Modern Art, New York (Acquired through the Lillie P Bliss bequest).

Projection systems

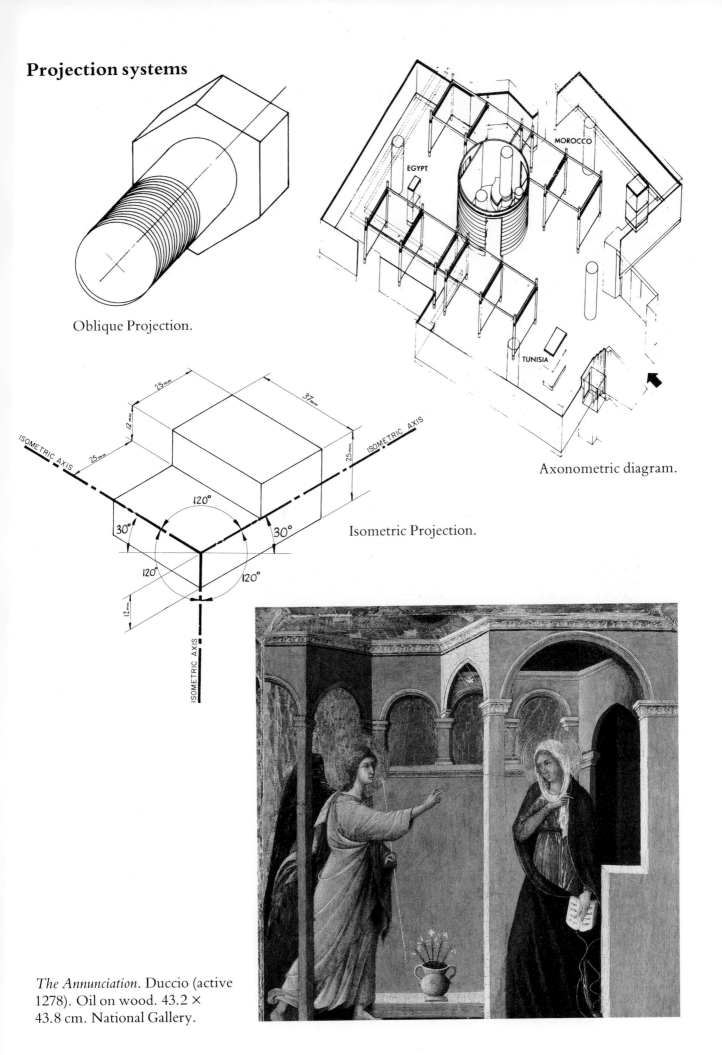

Oblique Projection.

Axonometric diagram.

Isometric Projection.

The Annunciation. Duccio (active 1278). Oil on wood. 43.2 × 43.8 cm. National Gallery.

Alexander the Great visits Queen Nushaba in the guise of an envoy, but she recognises him from his portrait. Tabriz style. c.1535–40. From a Persian manuscript of the Khamsa (five Poems) of Nizami. British Library.

Returning Sails at Shinagawa.
Suzuki Harunobu. 1764–70.
Woodblock print. 29.1 × 21.3 cm.
British Museum.

The Second Marriage. David
Hockney. 1963. Oil on canvas.
198 × 229 cm. Presented by the
Contemporary Art Society,
London, 1965. Reproduced by
permission of the National
Gallery of Victoria, Melbourne,
Australia.

Cross section diagram of a space shuttle. Science Photo Library.

Chiaroscuro

The Supper at Emmaus. Michaelangelo Merisi da Caravaggio (1573–1610). Oil on canvas. 141 × 196.2 cm. National Gallery.

Formal

Pattern

Aim

To design and print a textile using figurative or non-figurative motifs and a limited colour range for a specific use, e.g. a summer dress, a furnishing fabric for a teenager's bedroom, curtains for a school hall.

Objectives

1 To gain experience of a design process.
2 To learn the sequential development from designing to either block or silk-screen printing.
3 To understand the principle of overprinting colours.
4 To look at the other visual elements of art and design as they appear in pattern, i.e. line, shape, tone, colour, texture, form.
5 To study the notion of pattern and appreciate the similarities and differences to be found in designs from various cultures and times.

Primary source material

Although the final design and print might be non-figurative it is probably sensible to begin this project with drawing from actual objects. Later the interests of the student and the design process itself might produce abstract motifs, but to begin without definite reference is to run the risk of students producing visual cliché.

Discussions with the students which allow for an expression of their personal interests may mean that different starting points will be required, in which case the students could begin to collect their own primary source material at an early stage and to discuss its potential with the teacher and their colleagues. If such were to be the case there might be collected in the art room, natural forms: flowers, grasses, dried plants, shells, stones, bones, fish, stuffed birds and animals as well as live ones; or man made objects: parts of machinery, studio and kitchen equipment, tools and implements, musical instruments, the insides of clocks and watches, radios, televisions, car engines and toys, printed, woven and knitted textiles.

After the analytical drawing there will be the need to simplify, to extract the shapes both positive and negative, which will be the pattern motif, and for decisions to be made about the form e.g. tessellation, grid, half drop, etc. Then the printing process could be undertaken.

Discussion

Why has the theme been selected?

1 Pattern as an assembly of identical or similar units is one of the visual elements of art and design and so is crucial to an understanding of the subject.
2 The topic is broad and allows for the individual selection of an area of study from a number of categories.
3 Pattern is a part of both representational and non figurative art and design and is used to communicate ideas and feelings as well as to decorate or be functional.
4 In addition to being an element of art and design there are links between pattern and the other arts, e.g. the organisation of a piece of music, a dance, a play, prose and poetry. We use pattern to help structure our lives.

The aim and objectives of the project should be explained and discussed.

1 What do we think of as pattern?
2 Where do we find pattern a) in nature, b) in man-made objects?
3 Which surfaces in the art room are patterned and why?
4 What assembly of objects in the room form patterns and why?
5 Which patterns do we know which are a) decorative, and b) functional?
6 Under what headings might we place different sorts of pattern?
7 In what ways is pattern used in art and design, e.g. pictorial organisation, visual rhyme, constructional, decorative?

Contextual Studies

Whilst the notion of pattern as part of the pictorial composition of drawings and paintings, the structure of other arts and of societies in general may well be discussed during this project, it is pattern as the visual organisation of identical or similar units which is the main focus in this instance.

In attempting to achieve the main aim of producing a textile design and print for a given purpose the students will look at a large number of pattern forms and productions in order to develop their own designs and make links between styles and functions.

Areas of Study

The following are some types of pattern which might be considered by student and teacher:
- natural pattern;
- man-made pattern;
- regular;
- irregular;
- intentional;
- unintentional;
- functional;
- decorative;
- representational;
- non-representational;

- geometric;
- non–geometric;
- symmetrical;
- asymmetrical;
- grids and tessellations;
- rotation;
- counterchange;
- half-drop, vertical and horizontal;
- full drop repeats.

In addition to looking at pattern from different countries and times it is worth considering the way in which pattern has been and is used in numerous areas of craft and design, e.g.
- ceramics;
- majolica;
- terra cotta;
- wood carving;
- carved ivories;
- jewellery;
- enamels;
- glass;
- stained glass;
- illuminated manuscripts;
- bookbinding;
- wrought ironwork;
- engraved and chased metalwork;
- engraved ornament;
- heraldry;
- basketry;
- mosaics;
- plasterwork;
- wallpaper design;
- printed and woven textiles, embroidery, lace, patchwork, etc.

Several of the mentioned areas of study may link together to form others. For instance, a pattern may be both decorative and functional, e.g in nature, plumage may be functional (keeping the bird warm) as well as decorative (attracting a mate). The same is to be found in human costume, adornment and decoration. There are also variations which relate to societies. The knitted construction of an Aran sweater is functional and decorative. In addition, the arrangement of the geometric units was originally created as identification in case of death at sea. In this case, both the functional and decorative elements of the pattern tell us something about the society from which it came.

Other forms of pattern for communication might be a part of a course. For example: signs and symbols such as roadsigns, heraldic, mystic and religious emblems. Extensions in visual research and contextual studies could include pattern in the environment, e.g. architecture, storage, stacking, display, grouping, garden and town planning, construction, advertising, typography, graphic and computer design.

Relationships between religions and pattern design could also be usefully studied, e.g. the non-figurative character of much Islamic and Jewish art. The role of women in pattern designing and the making of such artefacts as fabrics, wallpapers, ceramics and other craft activities involving pattern are further possibilities for contextual studies.

Aspects of the theme

Natural

Tropical trees.

Snowflake. Photograph by Jan Hinsch. Science Photo Library.

Man-made

Notes on Women's Conduct – Stretching Fabric. Utagawa Kuniyoshi (1797–1861). Woodblock (triptych print). 36.5 × 24 cm (each section). British Museum.

Ceiling at Kensington Palace.
Crown copyright. Reproduced
with the permission of the
Controller of HMSO.
Department of the Environment
Photographic Library.

Regular

Aran sweater.

Irregular

Eight Deer at Completion of His Conquests. Page from the Codex Zouche-Nuttal. Mexican. c.1350–1500. British Museum.

Intentional

Oba King with Two Attendants. Benin Bronze. c. Sixteenth century. Museum of Mankind.

50

trata, Portugal.

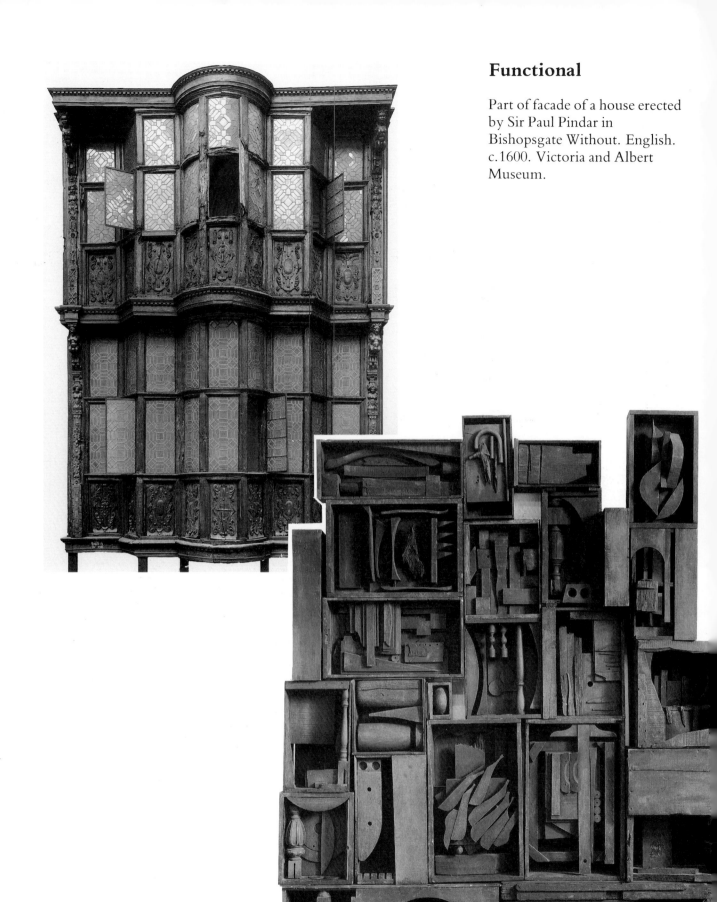

Functional

Part of façade of a house erected by Sir Paul Pindar in Bishopsgate Without. English. c.1600. Victoria and Albert Museum.

Decorative

Black Wall. Louise Nevelson. 1959. Black paint on wood. 264.2 × 216.5 ×64.8 cm. Tate Gallery, London.

Symmetrical

Nasca textile with bird design. Peru. c.200–100 BC. Museum of Mankind.

Asymmetrical

Birds Eating Banana. Elinus Cato. Grenada. Oil on canvas. Commonwealth Institute.

Representational

Cockatoo and Pomegranate. Walter Crane wallpaper design. 1899. Whitworth Art
Gallery, University of Manchester.

Non-representational

Geometric

Carpet page with cross from the Lindisfarne Gospels. Before AD 698. 34.3 × 24.8 cm. British Library.

Holiday apartments, France.

Non-geometric

Isnik ware dish. Turkey. Late sixteenth century. Large dish painted in red, blue and green on white ground under clear glaze. Diameter: 28 cm. Victoria and Albert Museum (Bridgeman Art Library).

Square and non-square grids

Tile mosaic from Rievaulx Abbey, Yorkshire. Thirteenth century. British Museum.

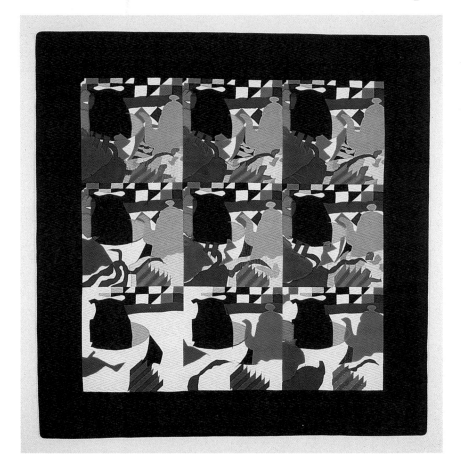

Pink Teapot. North American patchwork quilt. Pauline Burbidge.

Counterchange

Kasai Velvet. Kuba, Zaire. Out-pile, raphia cloth. 128 × 50 cm. British Museum.

Rotation

Permutation of Five. Mary
Martin. 1967. Stainless steel and
painted wood on formica and
wood. 49.5 × 49.5 × 10 cm.
Estate Mary Martin, courtesy
Annely Juda Fine Art.

Vertical half-drop

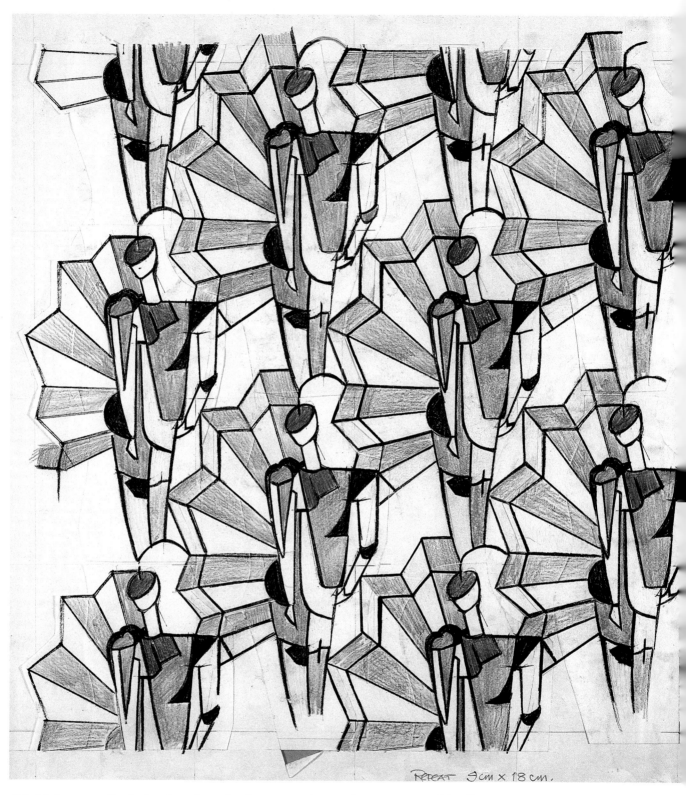

A half-drop textile design based on the fragmentation and movement of the figure and related to the ideas of the Russian Constructivists. Stephanie Parkin. 1985. Coloured crayon, conté and collage. Repeat 9 × 18 cm. Courtesy of the artist.

Imaginative

Dreams

Aim

To make a number of studies of actual people, objects and locations and use these to compose a picture in a chosen medium which shows a moment, or a sequence of moments, from an experienced dream.

Objectives

1 To select visual images and organise them into a unified composition.
2 To understand the importance of analytical drawing.
3 To use observation as a basis for imaginative work.
4 To appreciate the relationships between colour, tone and mood.
5 To study how other artists, designers and craftspeople have interpreted the subject.

Primary source material

Resourcing this theme might, on first glance, appear to be impossible. However, the students' own experiences and their memory will provide a starting point. This is not to suggest that work on the theme should be undertaken solely on the basis of memory and imagination. It would seem sensible that, after discussing individual dreams, and the similarities and differences of experience between the members of the group, each person should list people, objects, locations, colours and sequences of events so that decisions may be made about what items to include in the final image or sequence of images. It might also be wise to stress at this stage that the aim of the project is to show a moment or a series of moments from a dream, not a whole dream in all its detail, which in all probability, would be impossible to remember.

Consequently, decisions will have to be made about which items to include in the final piece. A number of working drawings and colour sketches will be needed if the student is to work out ideas and make intelligent decisions. Drawings of the selected items, locations (the same or similar to those witnessed in the dream) and people (who either appeared or will serve to act as 'stand-ins'), will need to be done so that there is a sound basis of reality on which to build the image of a dream.

Discussion

Why has the theme been selected?

1 Dreams are a part of our experience of living and, because they are different from everyday reality, fascinate most people.
2 Many cultures at various times in their history have linked events, prophesies, future action and religion to dreams.
3 Dreams relate to our interest in the impossible, the supernatural, the fantastic, the macabre, fear and gratification which we experience through all the arts and the media.
4 The topic allows for images to be produced which, whilst being based on the real world, extend the imagination of both artist and viewer.

The aim and objectives of the project should be explained and discussed.

1 What parts of our dreams do we recall most clearly?
2 Why might this be so?
3 Who dreams in colour and who in black and white? What can we remember about the colours and about black and white images?
4 Where do we find images of dreams, e.g. Surrealist art, book covers, film posters, record sleeves, comics, advertisements?
5 Discuss the similarities and differences between a selection of images collected before the lesson.
6 Which of these pictures arrest our attention, convey a mood, excite an emotion and how have the artists and designers attempted to convey their ideas?
7 Do any images being discussed present a stereotyped picture of the theme? If so, how and why has this been done?

Contextual Studies

The purpose of this project is to allow for an imaginative response to the theme in conjunction with contextual research. This may be organised so that initially the students are asked to make an expressive response to an experienced dream and to discuss the different images and the success with which they have been able to express their ideas. Following on from this, they could be asked to make analytical drawings and colour studies of people, objects and locations in order to express in a more organised way a selected aspect of the theme. Consideration could be given to other artists' expressive and formal, figurative and abstract interpretations of the theme, e.g. Kokoshka, de Chirico, Dali and Klee.

Investigation into the ways in which artists have used dreams as part of their work in the past might range from African, Hindu, Islamic and Christian art to the Surrealist movement of the twentieth century. Links with popular culture in many lands and the different elements of the mass media will also be important.

Areas of Study

An imaginative study of the theme could include:
- happy dreams;
- nightmares;

60

- daydreams;
- visions;
- humour;
- reality in dreams;
- fantasy in dreams;
- dreams and the future;
- dreams and desire;
- dreams and fear;
- dreams in advertising;
- dreams and ideas of Utopia;
- the unusual juxtaposition of the familiar;
- Surrealism.

Aspects of the theme

Dream landscapes and figures

Landscape from a Dream. Paul Nash. 1938. Oil on canvas. 76 × 116 cm. Tate Gallery, London (Bridgeman Art Library).

The Ghost of a Flea. William Blake. c.1819–20. Tempera on wood. 21.5 × 16 cm. Tate Gallery, London.

Intensified reality

Os Ilyaque. Leonor Fini. c.1948.
Oil on canvas. 37 × 45 cm.
Christie's London. (Bridgeman
Art Library).

Reversions of scale

The Listening Room. René
Magritte. 1952. Oil on canvas.
45 × 55 cm. Private collection
(Bridgeman Art Library).

Eine Kleine Nachtmusik.
Dorothea Tanning. 1946. Oil on
canvas. 41 × 61 cm. Private
Collection (Bridgeman Art
Library).

Max Ernst and Dorothea
Tanning. Arizona, 1946.
Photograph by Lee Miller.
© Lee Miller Archives, 1985.

Film still from *The Incredible Shrinking Man*. Agreement for permission to reproduce stills between MCA Publishing Rights and Longman Education dated January 9, 1990.

Unusual juxtapositions

A Siren in Full Moonlight. Paul Delvaux. 1940. Oil on wood. 111.9 × 180 cm. Southampton Art Gallery.
© Foundation P. Delvaux – St Idesbald/Belgium and DACS 1990.

Visions

The Vision after the Sermon. Paul Gauguin. 1888. Oil on canvas. 73 × 92 cm. National Gallery of Scotland (Bridgeman Art Library)

Supernatural

Spirit House and Poster. Songkhla, Thailand.

Happiness

Bouquet with Flying Lovers. Marc Chagall. c.1934–47. Oil on canvas. 130.5 × 97.5 cm. Tate Gallery, London.

Religion

Illustration from *Paradise Lost*. Gustave Doré. 1861. 23.6 × 19 cm.

Messages

Illustration from *A Midsummer Night's Dream*, published in 1914. W. Heath Robinson.

Nightmare

'He falls into the Abyss head downwards' from The Temptation of St. Anthony. Odilon Redon. Lithograph. Victoria and Albert Museum.

Fear

The Gates of Hell. Auguste Rodin. c.1884. Bronze. Photographie Giraudon.

Gratification

The Garden of Earthly Delights (centre panel). Oil on wood. 220 × 195 cm. Hieronymous Bosch. The Prado, Madrid. (Bridgeman Art Library).

Humour

Illustration from *Alice through the Looking Glass*. Sir John Tenniel. c.1872. Victoria and Albert Museum.

Illustration from *A Midsummer Night's Dream*, published in 1914. W. Heath Robinson.

Stories

Rosei Dreams of Shinagawa. Kikugawa Eizan. c.1820. Woodblock print. 36.5 × 25.5 cm. British Museum.

Little Nemo in Slumberland. Winsor McKay. 22 October 1905.

Social

Parades

Aim

To design and construct a part of a clay relief panel based on the theme.

Objectives

1 To learn to discuss, contribute and work as one of a group.
2 To solve the problems of translating drawings into a constructed form.
3 To experience working in the third dimension with clay.
4 To learn the process of either firing or casting.
5 To research into the subject and gain an understanding of the social, political and cultural reasons for parades, as well as the visual forms in which they are represented.

Primary source material

It may not be possible to study a parade at first hand at the desired moment. There may not be a fortuitous procession passing, a happy coincidence occurring as you start work on the theme. But it might be possible for students to look at small happenings which are similar, e.g. Girl Guide and Boy's Brigade church parades, a local demonstration, a religious or political event. Such occasions are not unfamiliar or infrequent and could provide a starting point. However, even without such an event to hand, the student will, in all probability, have some experience of the subject and will be able to contribute to a discussion. It will be possible to consider how people process by observing dinner queues and ways of leaving playgrounds and social assemblies.

Looking at a large number of images on the theme will be an essential part of this project before a decision will be possible about what type of parade is to be depicted and whether or not it is to be specifically related to the students' experience and beliefs or an issue which is a matter of common concern. Practical consideration should also be given to the purpose of the frieze, its materials, structure and placement.

The fact that the project is in essence a figure composition will mean that students will participate as 'actors' or models, so that drawings of people and costumes, action and gesture may be produced as studies for the final piece. There will also be the need to draw in order to collect information for later translation into the third dimension; as well as to produce studies which show how individual sections of the frieze are composed as a unit whilst still relating to the form of the whole. The structural problems of assembling a modelled frieze will have to be addressed as will decisions about size and firing or casting. The use of colour, or its absence, will also have to be decided.

Discussion

Why has the theme been selected?

1 Parades are a human activity related to celebration and protest demonstration and therefore experienced either first or second-hand by most people.
2 The theme allows for a study of the context of parades in different countries and societies.
3 The sequential character of a passing parade gives an opportunity for a group project which will allow students to be responsible for part of a larger creation.
4 There are links with other visual and performing arts, social and group activities which may be explored. For example, the famous Diaghilev production of *Parade* 1917, designed by Pablo Picasso, scenario by Jean Cocteau, with music by Erik Satie as well as operas, dances, circuses, films, fêtes and musical parades.

The aim and objectives of the project should be explained and discussed.

1 What do we understand by the word 'parade' and what examples can we give?
2 Have any of the group taken part in a parade? If so, descriptions could be asked for. This might also include comments from others who had seen a parade, but not taken part in the event.
3 What are the reasons for people organising parades, e.g celebration, commemoration, entertainment, religious ritual and protest?
4 How has the linear nature of a parade been presented in the visual arts, e.g. performance, sculptural frieze, embroidered panel, long sequence of paintings or by the criss-crossing of a single picture-plane?
5 A passing parade is a sequence of images and events. How might these be shown in the group's relief sculpture?
6 Such sequential movement implies time. How can the idea of time be expressed in an exploration of the theme?
7 What will be the purpose of the frieze, what will it depict and why? In addition to people, or even in place of them, the construction could show animals, mechanical and non-mechanical vehicles and changing locations.

Contextual Studies

This project gives the opportunity to work on a cooperative endeavour from initial discussion and preliminary sketches through design to the final piece of construction. In conjunction with this there is the possibility for studying the working methods and procedures of people participating in similar group activities, e.g. medieval stone masons, Caribbean carnival float and costume makers. There will also be the necessity of researching into the cultural, social, religious and political purposes of parades.

Areas of Study

Parades could be put in the following categories:
- celebration;
- commemoration;
- entertainment;
- religious ritual;
- protest march.

Within these broad categories could be studied details such as:
- national days;
- independence days;
- May Day;
- coronations;
- military parades;
- Olympic processions;
- weddings;
- funerals;
- circuses;
- village fêtes;
- Caribbean carnivals;
- Rio carnival;
- Chinese New Year;
- strike and work marches.

Aspects of the theme
Celebration

Poster for the Lord Mayor's Show, London. London Transport.

Wimbledon F.A. Cup Winners, 1988. Photograph by Peter Francis (Camera Press).

Triumph of Caesar. Mantegna. 1485–94. Tempera on linen. 271.8 × 284.5 cm. Reproduced by Gracious Permission of Her Majesty the Queen.

Film still from *Quo Vadis* showing triumph of Caesar. © Turner Films (Photo: National Film Archive).

Decoration

Riders of the Panathenaic Procession. Parthenon frieze (detail). British Museum (Photo: Michael Holford).

Greek vase showing a horse race. 500–480 BC. British Museum (Photo: Michael Holford).

Commemoration

Remembrance Day Parade. 1951.

Religious ritual

Assumption Day Procession. Paros, Greece. 1962.

Temporal ritual

Procession of the Chinese (in fact, Koreans). Kondo Kiyonobu. Woodblock print with hand colouring. 32.5 × 55.5 cm. British Museum.

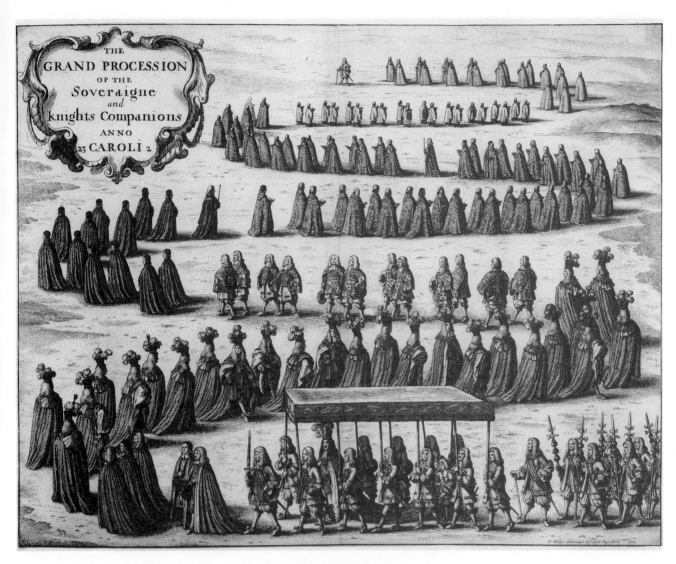

The Grand Procession, from the Institution Laws and Ceremonies of the Most Noble Order of the Garter.
Wenceslaus Hollar. 1672. Engraving. 29.8 × 37.5 cm. The British Museum.

Protest

Women's War Work Procession
passing through Piccadilly
Circus 17 July 1915. Museum of
London.

The Arrival of the Jarrow Marchers in London, 1936. T.C. Dugdale. Oil on canvas. Geffrye Museum.

Easter Parade

Easter Parade. Battersea Park,
London (Photo: Brian Shuel).

Fête

Fête in St. Rémy de Provence,
France.

National parades

Trooping the Colour. William Roberts. 1958–9. Oil on canvas. 183 × 274.3 cm. Tate Gallery, London.

May Day Parade, Moscow. 1978. Photograph by V. Koshevoi (Camera Press).

Coronation

Coronation of George VI. May 1937. Hulton Deutsch Collection.

The Speaker's Coach
This was used as the State
Coach until 1761.

MEXICO : Señor Don Primo Villa Michel.
NEPAL : Commanding-General Sir Kaiser Shumshere Jung Bahadur Rana, General Narayan Shumshere Jung Bahadur Rana, Colonel Surendra Shumshere Jung Bahadur Rana.
NETHERLANDS : Their Royal Highnesses Princess Juliana and Prince Bernhard.
NICARAGUA : Señor Dr. Don Constantino Herdocia.
NORWAY : Their Royal Highnesses the Crown Prince and Crown Princess.
PANAMA : Señor Dr. Don Arnulfo Arias.
PARAGUAY : Señor Dr. Don Rogelio Espinoza.
PERU : Señor Don A. Benavides.
POLAND : Colonel Beck, Vice-Admiral Unrug, M. Michael Moscicki.
PORTUGAL : Senhor Dr. Armindo Rodriques de Sttau Monteiro, General Domingos de Oliveira.
RUMANIA : His Royal Highness the Crown Prince.
SALVADOR : Señor Don Raul Contreras.
SAN MARINO : Mr. M. A. Jamieson.
SAUDI ARABIA : His Royal Highness the Emir Saud, Sheikh Yussuf Yasin.
SIAM : His Royal Highness Prince Chula Chakrabongs.
SOVIET UNION : M. Litvinoff, M. Maisky, Marshal Tukhachevsky.
SWEDEN : Their Royal Highnesses the Crown Prince and Crown Princess.
SWITZERLAND : M. Paravicini.
TURKEY : General Ismet Inonu, Admiral Sukru Okan.
UNITED STATES : Mr. James W. Gerard, General Pershing, Admiral Hugh Rodman.
URUGUAY : Señor Dr. Don Luis Alberto de Herrera.
VENEZUELA : Señor Dr. Don Caracciolo Parra-Perez.
YEMEN : Seif-al-Islam Husein.
YUGOSLAVIA : Their Royal Highnesses Prince Paul and Princess Olga.

* * *

Carriage Procession of Prime Ministers, Representatives of India and Burma, and Colonial Rulers

(Leaving Buckingham Palace at 9.15 a.m.)

1st Carriage
The Prime Minister of the United Kingdom, Rt. Hon. Stanley Baldwin, and Mrs. Baldwin.
Escort of Metropolitan Mounted Police.

2nd Carriage.
The Prime Minister of the Dominion of Canada, Rt. Hon. W. L. Mackenzie King, C.M.G.
Escort of Royal Canadian Mounted Police.

3rd Carriage.
The Prime Minister of the Commonwealth of Australia, Rt. Hon. J. A. Lyons, C.H., and Mrs. Lyons.
Australian Mounted Escort.

4th Carriage.
The Prime Minister of the Dominion of New Zealand, Rt. Hon. M. J. Savage.
New Zealand Mounted Escort.

5th Carriage.
The Prime Minister of the Union of South Africa, General the Rt. Hon. J. B. M. Hertzog.
South African Mounted Escort.

6th Carriage.
Sir Muhammad Zafrullah Khan (India) and Dr. Ba Maw (Burma).
Escort of Indian Cavalry.

7th Carriage.
The Prime Minister of Southern Rhodesia, Hon. G. M. Huggins, F.R.C.S., and Mrs. Huggins.
Southern Rhodesian Mounted Escort.

8th Carriage.
The Prime Minister of Northern Ireland, Rt. Hon. Viscount Craigavon, D.L.
Escort of Royal Ulster Constabulary.

9th Carriage.
The Sultan of Negri Sembilan.
The Sultan of Pahang.
The Sultan of Trengganu.
Escort of Troopers of the 16th/5th Lancers.

10th Carriage.
The Sultan of Johore.
Escort of Troopers of the 16th/5th Lancers.

11th Carriage.
The Sultan of Zanzibar and the Amir Abdullah of Transjordan.
Escort of Troopers of the 16th/5th Lancers.

* * *

CARRIAGE PROCESSION OF THE ROYAL FAMILY

(Leaving Buckingham Palace at 9.50 a.m.)
First Division, Captain's Escort.

1st Carriage—Glass Coach.
Her Royal Highness the Princess Royal.
Her Royal Highness Princess Elizabeth.
Her Royal Highness Princess Margaret.
Lord Lascelles.

2nd Carriage—Glass Coach.
Her Royal Highness the Duchess of Gloucester.
Her Royal Highness the Duchess of Kent.
The Hon. Gerald Lascelles.

3rd Carriage—State Landau.
Major.-General his Royal Highness Prince Arthur of Connaught, K.G., K.T., G.C.M.G., G.C.V.O., C.B.E.
Her Royal Highness Princess Arthur of Connaught.
Her Royal Highness Princess Alice, Countess of Athlone.

Second Division, Captain's Escort.

* * *

CARRIAGE PROCESSION OF HER MAJESTY QUEEN MARY

(Leaving Marlborough House at 10.10 a.m.)
First Division, Captain's Escort.

Glass Coach.

HER MAJESTY QUEEN MARY
Her Majesty the Queen of Norway.

Second Division, Captain's Escort, with Standard.

State Landau conveying Suite.

Page from official souvenir programme of the coronation of George VI. May 1937.

Carnival

Caribbean Carnival. Photograph by Sally and Richard Greenhill.

Chinese Dragon Dance. Photograph by Sally and Richard Greenhill.

Theatre parades

Start of the circus, in a bullring.

'Parade', Final Curtain for the Ballet. Pablo Picasso. 1917. Tempera on canvas. 1060 × 1724 cm. © Centre G. Pompidou. Musée National D'Art Moderne, Paris (Photo: Philippe Migeat).

Military

Bastille Day. 14 July, Paris.

Sport

Olympic Parade. Seoul, Korea. 1988. Photograph by Deutsch Press-Agentur GmbH (Camera Press).

Entertainment

Pied Piper of Hamlyn. Sutapa Biswas. Camden Arts Centre. Arkwright Arts Trust (Photo: Gareth Winters).

Afterword

There are certain educational issues, arising as they do from time to time, which provoke thought and even argument; perhaps not the heated debate which some propositions incite, but nonetheless sufficient interest for strong opinions to be voiced and individual stands taken. Contextual Studies in Art and Design is such a topic. Questions are asked, quite rightly, by teachers already under considerable pressure, about whether or not there is a place for the theoretical aspects of art and design in the syllabus. 'Is this another name for Art History?' 'Surely, not yet one more subject to add to an over-crowded timetable?' Then, perhaps more cynically, there is the comment that a new fashion is upon us, or worse, an old one has been revived.

We are all aware that most of the teaching which takes place in the school art room at present has a strong bias in favour of the practical. Artefacts are produced and emphasis placed on observation, analysis and interpretation. Such an approach has much to recommend it but is it a true visual education? Where is the broader historical, sociological, cross-cultural context? How often is there concern for a critical understanding of those aspects of the subject which do not fall within the Western European Fine Art tradition: craft, architecture, industrial design, fashion, film, television and advertising?

Surely such an approach to our subject is limited and restricts the aesthetic development of us all. Art education is not simply about the acquisition of a manual or even perceptual skill, but is a wider area of study capable of enriching not only the potential practitioner, but those who wish to have an informed appreciation of the environment, the different media of visual communication, their own past culture and that of others.

It is insufficient to limit the young person in school to the narrow confines of our own education and interests. We must stretch out in order to enrich the lives of our pupils, to enable them to see what it is they create in relation to that which has been created in the past, is being produced at present; and to assist in the appreciation and intelligent critical understanding of what is and has been important to societies other than our own.

A truly visual education is not only about making artefacts, studying the environment, expressing feelings. These are important aspects, germane to the development of us all, but for our full intellectual and aesthetic growth we rely also on a knowledge of cultural relevance, an appreciation of past achievement and an understanding of current ideas and initiatives.

If we are to grow and extend ourselves educationally we must be capable of placing what we see and what we make within the wider context. We should be able to make relationships across subjects, across art forms, across cultures and so establish links between the different visual and aesthetic elements of our experience. We must think, look, make...and think again.

...you've seen the world
...The beauty and the wonder and the power,
The shapes of things, their colours, lights and shades,
Changes, surprises...
What's it all about?
To be passed over, despised or dwelt upon.
Wondered at? Oh this last of course!...you say.

From 'Fra Lippo Lippi'
By Robert Browning

This afterword was first printed in 'Art History and Criticism in Schools', an account of a course for teachers run by the ILEA Art and Design Inspectorate, the Schools Sub-Committee of the Association of Art Historians and the University of London, Institute of Education.

Book List

Berger, J., *Ways of Seeing*, BBC, London, 1972

Boorstin, D., *The Image*, Penguin, 1961

Bronowski, J., *The Ascent of Man*, London, 1974

Burkhardt, T., *Art of Islam: Language and Meaning*, World of Islam Festival Trust, 1976

Clark, K., *Civilisation, A Personal View*, BBC & John Murray, 1969

El-Said, I., & Parman, A., *Geometric Concepts in Islamic Art*, Scorpion, 1988

Gombrich, E., *The Story of Art*, Phaidon, 1950

Gombrich, E., *Reflections on the History of Art*, Phaidon, 1987

Leach, B., *Beyond East and West*, Faber 1978

Loeb, H., Slight, P., & Stanley, N., *The Visual Arts in Multicultural Education* School of Oriental and African Studies, London, 1984

Martineau, J., & Hope, C., *The Genius of Venice 1500–1600*, Royal Academy of Arts, London, 1983

Moholy-Nagy, S., *Matrix of Man: an Illustrated History of the Urban Environment*, Pall Mall Press, 1968

Palmer, F., *Encyclopaedia of Oil Painting Materials and Techniques*, Batsford, 1984

Palmer, F., *Themes and Projects in Art and Design*, Longman, 1988

Palmer, F., *Visual Elements of Art and Design*, Longman, 1989

Pevsner, N., *The Englishness of English Art*, Architectural Press, 1956

Rewald, J., *History of Impressionism*, Secker & Warburg

Rewald, J., *Post-Impressionism*, Secker & Warburg

Shattuck, R., *The Banquet Years: The Origins of the Avant Garde in France, 1885 to the First World War*, Faber, 1955

Smith, M., ed., *The Artist in Tribal Society*, Royal Anthropological Institute, 1961

Sutton, P., *Masters of Seventeenth Century Dutch Genre Painting*, Philadelphia Museum of Art & The Royal Academy of Arts, London, 1984

Taylor, R., *Broadening the Context*, CSAE Occasional Publication No. 1, Schools, Arts & Crafts Councils 1982

Taylor, R., *Educating for Art: Critical Response and Development*, Longman, 1986

Tickner, L., *The Spectacle of Women: Imagery of the Suffrage Campaign 1907–14*, Chatto & Windus, 1987

Wickmann, S., *Japonisme*, Thames & Hudson, 1981

Slides

A number of slide-folios based on the visual elements are available from Rickitt Educational Media, Ilton, Ilminster, Somerset, e.g.

Natural Line
Man-made Line
Verticals and Horizontals
Shape
Squares and Rectangles
Surfaces

Repetition
Regular Pattern
Irregular Pattern
Optical Texture
Tactile Texture